Muddle Farm

Tasha Pym

Illustrated by Anni Axworthy

I went to Muddle Farm.

All the dogs said **Quack!**

All the ducks said **Woof!**

Woof!

All the horses said **Cluck!**

Cluck!

All the chickens said **Neigh!**

Neigh!

All the cows said **Baaa!**

Baaa!

All the sheep said **Mooo!**

Mooo!

I went to tell the farmer.

He said . . .

Cock-a-doodle-doo!